Jörg Sasse

5671, 1996
c-print face mounted on acrylic
106 x 180 cm
edition of 6
courtesy Galerie Wilma Tolksdorf, Frankfurt

Anna Gaskell

Untitled Number 5 (Wonder Series), 1996
laminated c-print mounted on board
127 x 101.5 cm
ed. 4/5
Private collection, London

Elisa Sighicelli

Las Vegas Curtain, 1997
partially backlit photograph
mounted on purpose-built light box
80 x 80 x 10 cm
ed. 1/3
courtesy the artist

Sarah Dobai

Couple, 1997
c-type print mounted on aluminium
71 x 86 cm
courtesy the artist

Miles Coolidge

Central Valley (near Stockton), 1997
c-print mounted on steel
26 x 330 cm
ed. 1/3
Private collection, London

Rineke Dijkstra

Buzz (Club) Liverpool, England, March 3, 1995
c-print
154 x 130 cm
courtesy Museum Boijmans Van Beuningen,
Rotterdam

Esko Männikkö

Martin, Batesville, (from the *Mexas* series), 1997
c-print in artist's frame
59 x 70 cm
ed. 2/20
courtesy Galerie Nordenhake, Stockholm

Rut Blees Luxemburg

Liebeslied, 1997
c-print mounted on aluminium
150 x 180 cm
ed. 1/2
courtesy Laurent Delaye Gallery, London

Jennifer Bornstein

Self Portrait with Senior Citizen, Farmer's Market,
3rd Street and Fairfax Avenue, Los Angeles
(from *Projector Stand 3* series), 1996
colour photograph
35.5 x 28 cm
ed. 3/6
courtesy Studio Guenzani, Milan

Paul Seawright

Untitled (from *The Missing* series), 1997
c-print mounted on aluminium
100 x 100 cm
ed. 3/6
courtesy Kerlin Gallery, Dublin

Hannah Starkey

Untitled, 1997
c-print mounted on aluminium and MDF
122 x 160 cm
ed. 3/3
courtesy the artist

Olafur Eliasson

Untitled (Ice Series), 1997
28 colour photographs
each 21.6 x 33.6 cm
ed. 1/3
Elizabeth and Alexander Stewart, Seattle;
courtesy Tanya Bonakdar Gallery, New York

Annika von Hausswolff

Attempting to Deal with Time and Space (No. VII),
1997
laminated c-print mounted on Dibond
110 x 80 cm
unique print from series of seven
Private collection, London

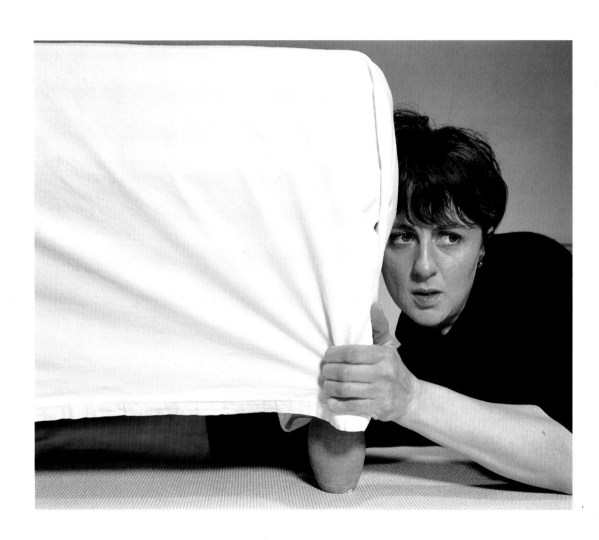

Florence Paradeis

Blank, May 1997
laminated c-print mounted on Dibond
146 x 180 cm
ed. 1/2
courtesy Galerie des Archives, Paris

the end is the beginning is the end
Simon Morrissey

It was a good day.

She picked up the book (it was a yellowing, schlocky seventies paperback about something or other) in an obvious attempt to delay the task at hand, and the disclaimer grabbed her before she could go any further:

This work is wholly fictional. Any resemblance to the objective present or past is gratuitous, and similarly resemblance to any actual event or character is accidental and not intended.

It was such an obvious deception that she assumed the author must have been using it as a device. She wondered if anyone really believed that it was possible for fiction to emerge from nowhere. No matter how fantastical the creation, how outlandish the construction, there was no getting away from the fact that everything has its root in reality (even if only as a composite of fragments compiled without really remembering where they sprang from).

She flicked on the TV. The news was in mid-flow pronouncing the truth about this or that. As the camera panned across a young woman sitting in a cafe, inconsequential behind the voice of the anchorman, it struck her that the opposite was also true. The things we burden with the authority of truth are surely as constructed as fiction. The very process of communicating experience automatically transforms them into an unstable state – a state that mimics reality almost perfectly but becomes ambiguous, lacking the certainties we expect from it.

Perhaps there really is no reliable state outside of a lived moment. The more she thought about it the more everything seemed to exist in a state of permanent flux, the ability to define any given state collapsing the more questions that were brought to bear against it.

The picture had turned to the panicky white snow of dead air and she hadn't even noticed.

*   *   *

It is now impossible to put forward any single reading with authority.

Some clichés are more helpful than others in this context, and one keeps resurfacing: increasingly there has been a collapse of consensus in society, whether it be in the area of politics, aspirations or social and gender definitions. It is as if, with the turn of the Millennium approaching, the idea of choice, if not the reality, has reached a critical mass. The subsequent pressure exerted on the old hegemonies has caused them to fragment, splintering into a myriad of new possibilities, creating many smaller, infinitely variable identities.

Within this pervasive atmosphere an intensified search for resonance has arisen. But as this need becomes stronger there seems to be an inverse deterioration in the ability to satisfy it. As this atmosphere collides with photography, our expectation of the medium's ability to render experience in all its immediacy, to interrogate meaning with a visceral intensity, is infected with the simultaneous awareness that certainties are now harder than ever to harness.

Jörg Sasse's photograph *5671* is located firmly within this unstable ground. Depicting a tower block shrouded in a skirt of grey fog, *5671* suspends a moment with precision, the building becoming a brutally-built ship in the process of levitating from the water. This ostensibly simple photograph is powerful exactly because of its clarity, its apparent lack of artifice in the rendering of experience.

When *5671* is seen with Sasse's other images, however, the possibility emerges that the photograph is not as it seems. Numbered as if from an inventory, Sasse's images range through the landscape, both domestic and magisterial, natural and man-made. As the viewer passes through the artist's pictorial universe there is a simultaneous sense of anonymity and déjà vu. This arises because Sasse does not actually take photographs himself, preferring instead to collate a secondary environment of found images. But the familiarity that could be expected from common-place sources disintegrates in Sasse's hands. Digitally rearranged and 'improved upon', elements of these stolen photographs suddenly sprout areas of hyper-realist painterly rendering, or a froth of pixellation applied to the most insignificant detail. Within this unpredictable context the previous impression of *5671*'s status begins to collapse – it too, despite its deceptive directness, has in fact been computer manipulated.

Although it forms an inevitable part of the discussion about Sasse's photography, it is not the fact that his images, or those of other contemporary photographers, are manipulated or constructed that is exceptional in itself – after all such tactics are as old as photography itself. What is important is that the popular awareness of photography as being open to falsification has created an uncertainty in our relationship with the image. The fact that computer technology is now so common-place has created a general recognition of how easy it is to alter a photograph. Old confidences are now no longer invested in the photograph so readily, because the most straight-forward image could be a complete fabrication. This has created a situation where the viewer vacillates between long-held assumptions about photography and new suspicions: between assuming the veracity of the photographic image and suspecting intervention in the image where there has probably been none.

The French anthropologist Marc Augé recently argued that the urban environment is increasingly dominated by certain spaces which he has termed 'non-places', that bear all the characteristics of being places yet lack the ability to create or possess meaning[1]. Similarly, photography's hybrid identity has de-stabilised the space between viewer and viewed. The flux of assumptions which now fills this space has produced a situation where the photographic image occupies a state resembling reality, yet lacks the ability to possess the certainties of the phenomenal world. Neither exclusively a device of record nor of creation, the photograph has become a 'non-reality', essentially ambivalent and unreliable, and possessed with a new autonomy from its consumers.

This open-endedness is charged with the particular energy that arises from the proximity of different forms, from the feeling that all modes of operation are equally possible and equally valid. Thus Rineke Dijkstra and Esko Männikkö's portraiture can exist beside Florence Paradeis or Sarah Dobai's staged events; Anna Gaskell's seductive fantasy next to Rut Blees Luxemburg's loaded urban landscapes; Jörg Sasse's manipulated landscape next to Paul Seawright's meticulously observed fragments of identity. Within the fluidity of positions now open to artists the possibility of movements or even theoretical schools dominating photographic practice seems increasingly implausible.

This new autonomy has, however, been firmly anchored in a return to essentials – in an attempt to convey the primacy and complexity of experience. In the face of the elusiveness of conclusions, artists have located their desire to scrutinise the way meaning is constructed and conveyed in arenas of familiarity: within the everyday, on the outskirts of our dominant fictions, and predominantly, within our own image.

The teenage girls out clubbing in Rineke Dijkstra's *Buzz* portraits are starkly isolated against their white background, the camera's scrutiny of the teenagers' awkward sexuality bordering on interrogation. While the artist appears to have created a harsh relationship between observer and subject she is far from condoning the authoritative gaze. Dijkstra attempts to go beyond cliché and judgement towards more unstable ground – the complexity of individual identity. In her candid framing Dijkstra preserves a single moment in the continual flux of influences, aspirations and personality that will be uniquely fused on each teenager's passage to individuality. The very explicitness of the artist's gaze, and her inclusion of the dichotomies that make up every individual, empowers each of Dijkstra's subjects with an autonomy equal to those that regard them. Behind the gawky surface of untutored make-up and little black dresses revealing too much of puppy-fat limbs, an embryonic self-assurance manifests itself as the teenagers claim the arena of the Buzz club for their own.

The autonomy of image and subject resounds within Esko Männikkö's portraits. Both Männikkö and Dijkstra exist within a strong tradition of celebrating the dignity of the individual that can be traced back through Diane Arbus to August Sander. In contrast to Dijkstra, however, Männikkö does not frame the individual exclusively, but imbues identity as much in the objects and environments that surround the people he portrays as in the individuals themselves. Männikkö lives amongst his often poor or isolated subjects before he photographs them, participating in their lives to a degree that almost makes the resultant images become the product of collaboration. The tattoo of the word 'beer' on Victoriano's hand; Martin cosseting his bird whilst wearing an 'Our Lady of Guadalupe' sweatshirt; the cheap painting of a child beauty-queen wedged in the window frame behind a sweat-stained man's head - these details are not forced to tell any pre-existing narrative but are allowed to simply exist within the continually shifting matrix of identity. Rather than offering conclusions Männikkö's images become thresholds in a looped dialogue of identity between subject and viewer.

The possibility exists that the more dislocated these details become, the more explicit their authority. Paul Seawright's series *The Missing* separates his images from any easily discernible context. But there is no escape from the message his heightened concentration on these fragments conveys. The poverty of the artist's images is at one with the harshness of his subjects' environment - the bare conjunction of a clothes rail and cheap shirt is almost barren of content, without any formal augmentation; a pair of dirt-ingrained hands are so closely focused as to betray social situation in the texture of skin and nail. There is an implicit surrender of the photographer's authority over his subject in Seawright's exclusion of the complete frame of the traditional portrait. Speculation about the circumstances or histories of his homeless and missing subjects is frustrated to a point where its end is located deliberately at the beginning of our engagement with the image. The anonymity afforded Seawright's subjects through his concentration on details alone allows the images to become breathing spaces within which the disenfranchised can defy the inequalities of categorisation.

As certainties within portraiture dissolve, they do so equally elsewhere. In his *Central Valley* series Miles Coolidge brings a meticulous observation to his investigation of landscape that unsettles our preconceived notions. The artist's earlier series *Safetyville* documented a depopulated model town built to one-third normal size to teach children safe behaviour. Coolidge emphasised the subtle incongruities of the miniature town's clash with its environment - a building sitting haphazardly on the pavement, grass pushing through what should be its foundations; skinny saplings reaching above the buildings as if they were full-grown trees. Setting out to find an antidote to this skewed urbanity Coolidge decided to depict the rural horizon in *Central Valley*. The area he chose, however, is dominated by agriculture, and the artist's images reveal it is as constructed as any urban environment. Reducing the horizon to painfully thin strips, his photographs are allowed only a shallow segment of sky, stripping them of any possible romanticism. Instead the landscape is reduced to a repetitive composition of details; the banal regularity of crop fields, the formulaic architecture of prefabricated farm buildings – all unceremoniously contained beneath the ever present spikes of electricity pylons. This is landscape as forensic record rather than evocation of the sublime, and the sheer scale of its uniformity is practically overwhelming.

Coolidge's very search for an unadulterated nature reveals that landscape is in itself a symbol, one which is persistently maintained in an attempt to find an embodiment of transcendence and a force free of man's pervasive influence. Olafur Eliasson's ephemeral installations and photographic series further exploit this desire to locate a sense of wonder in nature. Just as the artist's installations produce spatial experiences with intimations towards the sublime through their combinations of light, water or fog, his untitled photographs of ice boulders marooned in the snow, toy with the desire for the existence of an unchanging, magisterial nature. Displayed in repetitive ranks reminiscent of the Bechers' studies of industrial architecture, Eliasson frames the ice as if it possesses a similar tension with the landscape. The boulders were the product of a volcanic eruption under Iceland's largest glacier, and despite their apparent solidity they melted quickly irrespective of being thousands of years old. In freezing with his camera what cannot remain in nature, Eliasson creates a 'non-reality' of the natural world more in tune with our appetite for permanence than with nature's inherent cycle of change and loss.

Sharon Lockhart composes the Japanese high-school students in her photographic series *Goshogaoka Girls Basketball Team* as blankly as Eliasson frames his ice boulders. Displayed in interdependent groupings, the images push the ability to communicate reliable meaning to its breaking point. The concept of time within the work has been paralysed. Arranged like illustrations in a step-by-step instruction manual and exquisitely formal, each figure attains the status of a mannequin in the glare of Lockhart's dramatic lighting. The information in the images is rendered with singular clarity and is immediately recognisable: the girls are engaged in acting out scenarios from a basketball game, and even each player's name is meticulously noted. The purpose of this explicitness remains perversely elusive, however. No clues are revealed in Lockhart's interdependent film *Goshogaoka*. Shot from a fixed position, the film operates at the other extreme of time, rendering the team's training as a seemingly endless duration of rhythmic acts without narrative. In both photographs and film, any conclusion is perpetually denied. Unable to attribute intention to the artist's unequivocal emphasis of detail, the meaning of Lockhart's intense study dissolves into abstraction before the impatience of our scrutiny.

Annika von Hausswolff's series *Attempting to Deal with Time and Space* feigns a similar directness in order to perpetrate a kind of confidence trick. In this apparently simple series of photographs showing the artist wrestling with an amorphous white balloon, the images' atmosphere moves from the playful to the anxious. As she struggles with the formless object, it is obvious that the balloon has the upper hand. Although the images are composed like a portrait, the balloon threatens to consume both the artist and the pictorial field. Becoming a substitute for Hausswolff's body, the balloon obscures her face and torso frustrating the viewer's attempt to identify her. Concealed behind what is essentially a tangible void, the artist thwarts our desire to consume her image. In its place Hausswolff inserts a metaphor for both our own inadequacy, and photography's inability, to fully bridge the gap between observer and observed.

Jennifer Bornstein's work consists of installations of films and photographs depicting herself in numerous social situations with different companions. Her images possess something of the comfortable informality of snapshots. Despite this familiarity, and her uncomplicated documentary style, there is a subtle deception at play which is so unconcealed as to almost evade its status as deceit. Drawing on her own distinctly flexible presence rather than artificial identities or disguise, Bornstein infiltrates a myriad of scenarios, confusing certainties of gender, age and personality as she does. By turns a boyish teenager hanging out with the boys at basketball courts and libraries, or a confident young woman caught on camera next to an old man at a vegetable stall, Bornstein is however always recognisably, and unnervingly, herself in each scenario. Bornstein appears to close the gap between herself and her companions by physically integrating with them. Yet the repeated, distinctive fixture of her presence eventually gives her project a disjunctiveness, underlining just how artificial this impression of community is.

Bornstein's deceit is therefore as fundamentally present as it is absent. Her work, like that of her contemporaries, is caught in a continuum between fiction and actuality where neither can assume the authority of being beginning or end, as both are equal partners within the image's existence. No matter how much we demand to know the nature of what we are engaging with, the photograph now refuses to offer any single conclusion, but instead lays open the flux of possibilities with a challenge that approaches defiance.

*   *   *

She is just sitting there, the white light of the interference skipping across her face.

The scene is from a mainstream horror film, nothing exceptional, from the late seventies or more probably the mid-eighties. She has an almost angelic face, framed by a long, roundish white-blond bob. She keeps staring into the television as if there is something there, her expression intent despite the lack of picture.

"Hallo" she says. She speaks with soft, rounded vowels. She keeps staring, more intently now, as if she is being addressed. " What do you look like?" she asks the interference, but there is no reply, no identification.

The light just dances in abstract patterns across her features.

*   *   *

Steadily a sense of déjà vu emerges, a sensation of familiarity without comprehension. A woman prepares a chicken for the oven; another fumbles under what appears to be a bed; a couple kiss. Florence Paradeis's ordinary moments are captured as if they were an antidote to spectacular occurrence, or at least of equal significance. The sense that Paradeis's project is a validation of the everyday disintegrates as their normality becomes troubled. The images are framed with a concentration that disrupts the normal flow of association and swells to become a creeping sense of directed theatricality. The deliberate accentuation of banal detail jars the images with a pregnancy that has no obvious place in their situations. These images tangibly threaten to implode under their own pressure, repelling the viewer as if they have succeeded in turning the ordinary into the grotesque.

The fact that Paradeis's images, and much other contemporary photography, suggest a greater narrative outside the photograph than they reveal within it, can lead the images to be labelled 'filmic'. This is not surprising when the moving images of cinema and television have become so pervasive that their power is at once inescapable and subliminal. Now the predominant visual influence on our lives, we are bathed in their glow almost unaware as they colonise our perception. Due precisely to this pervasiveness the use of filmic metaphors in the discussion of contemporary photography has become, to a large extent, a critical shorthand where simply to invoke the cultural weight of cinema is in itself presented as an explanation of a photograph's potency.

Although Anna Gaskell's *Wonder Series* draws both on the mechanisms and the visual seduction of cinema, it would be too simple an analysis to suggest that this is the source of the images' peculiar strength. Constructed with actors, costumes and lighting, Gaskell's images are a re-interpretation of Lewis Carroll's *Alice in Wonderland* narrative as if from a series of stills from an un-made film. Rendered giddily seductive through vivid colour and the intimacy of the camera to its subjects, the photographs indulge in all the sensory richness possible in photography, immersing the viewer in an immediate world of sensation. Beneath their surface, however, a darker potential infects the *Wonder Series*. Co-existing with the images' seductive appearance is a fluctuating subtext of cruelty and unease. A girl holds the nose of another and forces her head back at an uncomfortable angle. Another girl has her mouth scrubbed out with soap. The fact that the girls are identical twins, and hence images of each other, suggests that the anxiety which insists on surfacing in Gaskell's images arises from a fear of the consequences implicit in confronting the self.

Popular cinema explicitly deals in defined narratives and in predetermined conclusions. Moments tend to exist upon a distinct trajectory and for distinct reasons. In spite of the similarities they share with film's staging, it would be a mistake to project cinematic metaphors onto the work of Sarah Dobai or Hannah Starkey. Devoid of any certainty of meaning, Sarah Dobai's prostrate couple are bathed in a sallow light, one figure apparently awake, one asleep. Nothing in their demeanour suggests this is anything but an approximation to the authenticity of a lived moment. But as in Dobai's other photographs, the figures are framed against a dense, enveloping blackness that obliterates all possibility of a context derived from location. The characters appear instead to be relating to some undefined stimulus outside of the picture, which could even be the equally disconnected figures in the artist's other images. Isolated within this shared vacuum there is no prospect of closure - only a continual tension and an unquantifiable, perpetual openness.

Hannah Starkey insists on withholding the possibility of narrative conclusion. Whether slumped on a chair in the aftermath of a party, returning from a shopping trip on the Underground or catching a moth against a café mirror, the women in Starkey's images only surrender a limited degree of information to the viewer. Neither explicitly constructed nor attempting to deceive the viewer that they are actual events, her photographs hover between the mundane and the transcendent with an ambiguity fed on the simultaneous presence of anticipation and loss. Suspended, Starkey's scenarios exist as suggestions of narratives that are inescapably imbued with their own inability to evolve.

The presentation of place itself can be pregnant enough without the potential of narrative. Elisa Sighicelli's uninhabited interiors resonate with an animation that at first appears indefinable. These unremarkable combinations of curtain and edge of bed, of chairs and table in the turn of a wall, suggest a continuation beyond their pictorial confines through the very palpability of the light that creeps into the deserted homes. This suggestion of the sublime wiithin the everyday is achieved by substituting a graduated artificial light for the depicted light at the window. By using light boxes the artist allows the multiplication of illusion to attain an almost tangible depth, transfixing the viewer in a slowly diffusing light.

In Rut Blees Luxemburg's photographs of the urban landscape the artist surrenders her authority over the photographic process in order to afford space itself the ability to defy containment. Actively courting this independence,

Luxemburg permits her palette to be dictated by the influence of environmental lighting on the long exposures she opens to the city. Drenched in the green-gold suspension of a nocturnal underpass, *Liebeslied* resounds with the potential to transcend its own definition. Concurrently brutal and beautiful, a resistance to consumption is active on every scale. At the rear of the stairwell a clump of black lines defines the site of meticulously obscured graffiti. As with the image itself, the graffiti has the potential to possess any meaning we may project onto it, and the certainty that we will never know its actual nature. The artist's identification of the graffiti as a love poem in the photograph's title only de-stabilises the image even further. As her suggestion can never be confirmed *Liebeslied* inevitably becomes the location of a perpetual loop of doubt.

There is a photograph on the wall in front of you. It is now impossible to put forward any single reading with authority. Flick a coin into the air. It spins, wobbling, ungainly and heavy above you....

*   *   *

It stops its drunken descent and comes to rest.
Moving as if through water she sweeps her hand slowly behind the moth. Then the wings are beneath her fingers, pinned there.
She stares at the intricate patterns on its back, the mirror a halo of refracted light from the sun, dancing like television interference through the cafe windows.

[a radio drifts by....end of a century....oh, it 's nothing special....]

It was going to be a good day.

Simon Morrissey 1997

1. Marc Augé,
*Non-Places: Introduction
to an Anthropology of
Supermodernity*, Verso,
London, 1995.

List of works

Jennifer Bornstein
Projector Stand 3, 1996
series of 5 colour photographs
each 28 x 35.5cm
ed. 3/6
courtesy Studio Guenzani, Milan

Miles Coolidge
Central Valley (near Stockton), 1997
c-print mounted on steel
26 x 330cm
ed. 1/3
Private collection, London

Miles Coolidge
Central Valley (near Lemoore), 1997
c-print mounted on steel
26 x 327.5cm
ed. 1/3
courtesy Casey Kaplan, New York
and Acme., Santa Monica

Rineke Dijkstra
*Buzz (Club) Liverpool, England,
March 3*, 1995
c-print
154 x 130cm
courtesy Museum Boijmans Van
Beuningen, Rotterdam

Rineke Dijkstra
*Buzz (Club) Liverpool, England,
March 4*, 1995
c-print
154 x 130cm
courtesy Museum Boijmans Van
Beuningen, Rotterdam

Rineke Dijkstra
Buzz (Club) Liverpool, England,

March 11, 1995
c-print
154 x 130cm
courtesy Museum Boijmans Van
Beuningen, Rotterdam

Sarah Dobai
Couple, 1997
c-type print mounted on aluminium
71 x 86cm
courtesy the artist

Sarah Dobai
Laughing Man, 1997
c-type print mounted on aluminium
86 x 71cm
courtesy the artist

Sarah Dobai
Conspirators, 1997
c-type print mounted on aluminium
71 x 86cm
courtesy the artist

Sarah Dobai
Untitled (Garden), 1997
c-type print mounted on aluminium
96.5 x 114.25cm
courtesy the artist

Olafur Eliasson
Untitled (Ice Series), 1997
28 colour photographs
each 21.6 x 33.6cm
ed. 1/3
Elizabeth and Alexander Stewart,
Seattle; courtesy Tanya Bonakdar
Gallery, New York

Anna Gaskell
Untitled Number 1 (Wonder Series),

1996
laminated c-print mounted on board
40.6 x 50.8cm
ed. AP/2
courtesy Nina Robbins and Frank
Moore, New York

Anna Gaskell
Untitled Number 2 (Wonder Series),
1996
laminated c-print mounted on board
127 x 101.5cm
ed. 1/5
courtesy Nina Robbins and Frank
Moore, New York

Anna Gaskell
Untitled Number 5 (Wonder Series),
1996
laminated c-print mounted on board
127 x 101.5cm
ed. 4/5
Private collection, London

Anna Gaskell
Untitled Number 8 (Wonder Series),
1996
laminated c-print mounted on board
76 x 101.5cm
courtesy Yvonne Force Inc., New York

Annika von Hausswolff
*Attempting to Deal with Time and
Space (No. I)*, 1997
laminated c-print mounted on Dibond
110 x 80cm
unique print from series of seven
courtesy Jan Widlund, Advokatfirman
Vinge, Stockholm

Annika von Hausswolff
Attempting to Deal with Time and Space (No. VI), 1997
laminated c-print mounted on Dibond
110 x 80cm
unique print from series of seven
courtesy Casey Kaplan, New York

Annika von Hausswolff
Attempting to Deal with Time and Space (No. VII), 1997
laminated c-print mounted on Dibond
110 x 80cm
unique print from series of seven
Private collection, London

Sharon Lockhart
Goshogaoka Girls Basketball Team: Chihiro Nishijima; Sayaka Miyamoto and Takako Yamada; Kumiko Shirai and Eri Hashimoto; Kumiko Kotake
95.2 x 377cm
(detail from a series of 12)
framed Chromogenic prints
ed. 3/8
Private collection, Cologne; courtesy neugerriemschneider, Berlin

Sharon Lockhart
Goshogaoka Girls Basketball Team: Ayako Sano, 1997
114.25 x 96.5cm
(detail from a series of 12)
framed Chromogenic prints
ed. 3/8
Private collection, Cologne; courtesy neugerriemschneider, Berlin

Rut Blees Luxemburg
Corporate Leisure, 1997
c-print mounted on aluminium
180 x 150cm
ed. 1/2
courtesy Laurent Delaye Gallery, London

Rut Blees Luxemburg
Silverblade, 1997
c-print mounted on aluminium
61 x 51cm
ed. 2/5
courtesy Laurent Delaye Gallery, London

Rut Blees Luxemburg
Liebeslied, 1997

c-print mounted on aluminium
150 x 180cm
ed. 1/2
courtesy Laurent Delaye Gallery, London

Esko Männikkö
Frank and Christina, San Antonio (from the *Mexas* series), 1996
c-print in artist's frame
96 x 116cm
ed. 5/20
courtesy Galerie Nordenhake, Stockholm

Esko Männikkö
Victoriano, Batesville (from the *Mexas* series), 1997
c-print in artist's frame
53 x 63cm
ed. 3/20
courtesy Galerie Nordenhake, Stockholm

Esko Männikkö
Untitled, Batesville (from the *Mexas* series), 1996
c-print in artist's frame
64 x 77cm
ed. 3/20
courtesy Galerie Nordenhake, Stockholm

Esko Männikkö
Martin, Batesville (from the *Mexas* series), 1997
c-print in artist's frame
59 x 70cm
ed. 2/20
courtesy Galerie Nordenhake, Stockholm

Esko Männikkö
Cowboy, San Antonio (from the *Mexas* series), 1996
c-print in artist's frame
77 x 93cm
ed. 3/20
courtesy Galerie Nordenhake, Stockholm

Florence Paradeis
Blank, May 1997
laminated c-print mounted on Dibond
146 x 180cm
ed. 1/2
courtesy Galerie des Archives, Paris

Florence Paradeis
La Cuisinière, December 1996
laminated c-print mounted on Dibond
diptych, each 113 x 90cm
ed. 1/2
courtesy Galerie des Archives, Paris

Florence Paradeis
Le Baiser, September 1996
laminated c-print
145 x 120cm
unique print
courtesy Collection Galerie du Jour Agnès B., Paris

Jörg Sasse
5671, 1996
c-print face mounted on acrylic
106 x 180cm
edition of 6
courtesy Galerie Wilma Tolksdorf, Frankfurt

Jörg Sasse
5502, 1996
c-print face mounted on acrylic
106 x 160cm
edition of 6
courtesy Galerie Wilma Tolksdorf, Frankfurt

Jörg Sasse
6137, 1996
c-print face mounted on acrylic
106 x 180cm
edition of 6
courtesy the artist and Galerie Wilma Tolksdorf, Frankfurt

Paul Seawright
Untitled (from *The Missing* series), 1997
c-print mounted on aluminium
150 x 150cm
ed. 2/6
courtesy Kerlin Gallery, Dublin

Paul Seawright
Untitled (from *The Missing* series), 1997
c-print mounted on aluminium
100 x 100cm
ed. 2/6
courtesy Kerlin Gallery, Dublin

Paul Seawright
Untitled (from *The Missing* series), 1997
c-print mounted on aluminium

100 x 100cm
ed. 3/6
courtesy Kerlin Gallery, Dublin
The Missing series, comprising 15 images, was commissioned by the Nederlands Foto Instituut, Rotterdam

Elisa Sighicelli
Curtain, 1997
partially backlit photograph mounted on purpose-built light box
80 x 80 x 10cm
ed. 1/3
courtesy the artist

Elisa Sighicelli
Table, 1997
partially backlit photograph mounted on purpose-built light box
80 x 80 x 10cm
ed. 1/3
courtesy the artist

Elisa Sighicelli
Las Vegas Curtain, 1997
partially backlit photograph mounted on purpose-built light box
80 x 80 x 10cm
ed. 1/3
courtesy the artist

Hannah Starkey
Untitled, 1997
c-print mounted on aluminium and MDF
122 x 160cm
ed. 3/3
courtesy the artist

Hannah Starkey
Untitled, 1997
c-print mounted on aluminium and MDF
122 x 160cm
ed. 3/3
courtesy the artist

Hannah Starkey
Untitled, 1997
c-print mounted on aluminium and MDF
122 x 160cm
ed. 3/3
courtesy the artist

Biographies

Jennifer Bornstein
Born Seattle, 1970. Lives and works in New York.

Selected Solo Exhibitions
1998: Blum & Poe, Santa Monica; greengrassi, London
1997: Studio Guenzani, Milan
1996: Blum & Poe, Santa Monica (project)

Selected Group Exhibitions
1997: *Her Eyes Are a Blue Million Miles*, Three Day Weekend, Malmö (curated by Dave Muller); *The Name of the Place*, Casey Kaplan, New York (curated by Laurie Simmons); *Exposition Collective de Jeunes Photographes Femmes*, Galerie Anne de Villepoix, Paris
1996: Three Day Weekend, P-House, Tokyo; *LACE Annuale*, Los Angeles Contemporary Exhibitions, Los Angeles (curated by Suzanne Ghez)
1995: *The Big Night* (for Colin Gardner), Bradbury Building, Los Angeles
1994: *Collectors' Favourites no. 56*, Cable Access Channel 3, Los Angeles

Miles Coolidge
Born Montreal, 1963. Lives and works in Los Angeles.

Selected Solo Exhibitions
1996: *Garage Pictures*, Casey Kaplan, New York; *Safetyville*, Acme., Santa Monica
1994: *Elevator Pictures*, Re: Solution Gallery, Los Angeles Centre for Photographic Studies, Hollywood

Selected Group Exhibitions
1997: *Stills: Emerging Photography in the 1990s*, Walker Art Centre, Minneapolis (curated by Douglas Fogle); *Model Terrains*, Carnegie Museum of Art, Pittsburgh
1996: *Skin Deep*, Thomas Solomon's Garage, Los Angeles (touring); *The Lie of the Land*, University Art Museum, University of California, Santa Barbara
1995: *Redevelopment*, Victoria Room, San Francisco
1994: *Rundgang*, Kunstakademie Düsseldorf

Rineke Dijkstra
Born Sittard, The Netherlands, 1959. Lives and works in Amsterdam.

Selected Solo Exhibitions
1997: Galerie Mot & Van den Boogaard, Brussels; Photographers' Gallery London,
1996: *Le Consortium*, Dijon; Galerie Paul Andriesse, Amsterdam
1995: Stedelijk Museum Bureau, Amsterdam (with Tom Claassen); *Time Festival, Rineke Dijkstra*, Museum of Contemporary Art, Gent (with Hugo Delbaere)

Selected Group Exhibitions
1997: *New Photography 13*, Museum of Modern Art, New York; *Future, Present, Past*, Biennale di Venezia; *Face to Face*, Nederlands Foto Institut, Rotterdam
1996: *Gemeente Aankopen 96*, Stedelijk Museum, Amsterdam; *Fotofiktion*, Kasseler Kunstverein, Kassel; *Prospect 96*, Schirn Kunsthalle, Frankfurt
1995: *A Europa e o Mar*, Encontros da Imagem, Braga, Portugal; *The European Face*, Talbot Rice Gallery, Edinburgh

Sarah Dobai
Born London, 1965. Lives and works in London.

Solo Exhibitions
1994: Rodney Graham's Studio exhibition project, Vancouver

Selected Group Exhibitions
1997: *SWEAT*, Camerawork, London (with Tony Tasset); *Knowledge/Control/Power*, Finnish Museum of Photography, Helsinki; *New Contemporaries*, Cornerhouse, Manchester (touring); *Experiment GB*, Kunstverein Trier and Kubus Gallery, Hanover; *B.c.c.*, Cleveland Street and The Tannery, London (curated by Andrew Renton)
1996: *Fifty Quid*, Derbyshire Street Arts

1995: *Wall to Wall*, Or Gallery, Vancouver

Olafur Eliasson
Born Hafnarfjordür, Iceland, 1967. Lives and works in Berlin.

Selected Solo Exhibitions
1997: Reykjavik Municipal Museum; Galerie neugerriemschneider, Berlin; The Curious Garden, Kunsthalle Basel
1996: *Your Foresight Endured*, Galleria Emi Fontana, Milan; *Your Strange Certainty Still Kept*, Tanya Bonakdar Gallery, New York
1995: Künstlerhaus, Stuttgart; *Thoka*, Hamburger Kunstverein, Hamburg

Selected Group Exhibitions
1997: *Truce*, Site-Santa Fe, Santa Fe (curated by Francesco Bonami); *New Scandinavian Art*, Louisiana Museum, Humlebaek, Denmark; Istanbul Biennial
1996: *Manifesta 1*, Rotterdam; *Prospect 96*, Frankfurt Kunstverein
1995: *Campo 95*, Venice, Turin, Malmö (curated by Francesco Bonami)

Anna Gaskell
Born Des Moines, Iowa, 1969. Lives and works in New York.

Solo Exhibitions
1997: Casey Kaplan, New York

Selected Group Exhibitions
1997: Opening Exhibition, *Installations/Projects* (with Dan Graham), PS1 Contemporary Art Centre, New York; *Stills: Emerging Photography in the 1990s*, Walker Art Centre, Minneapolis (curated by Douglas Fogle); *Summer Exhibition*, Galerie Anne de Villepoix, Paris; *Making Pictures: Women in Photography, 1975-Now*, Bernard Toale Gallery, Boston in association with Nicole Klagsbrun
1996: *Portraiture*, White Columns,

New York; *Unreal*, Hope 57, New York; *Baby Pictures*, Bravin Post Lee, New York
1995: *Currents*, The Eighth Floor, New York

Annika von Hausswolff
Born Gothenburg, 1967. Lives and works in Stockholm.

Solo Exhibitions
1997: Andréhn-Schiptjenko, Stockholm

Selected Group Exhibitions
1997: *Popular Mechanics*, Hollywood Premiere, Los Angeles; *Funny Versus Bizarre*, Contemporary Art Centre, Vilnius and Modern Art Museum, Riga
1996: Bienal de São Paulo; *Stay on your own for slightly longer*, Transmission Gallery, Glasgow; *Till Filmen*, Göteborgs Konstmuseum; *(a:t) technology, internet project*, http://sunsite.kth.se/art
1995: *BOREALIS 7 - Desire*, Nordiskt Konstcentrum, Finland and Louisiana Museum, Humlebaek, Denmark

Sharon Lockhart
Born Norwood, Massachussetts, 1964. Lives and works in Los Angeles.

Selected Solo Exhibitions
1998: Blum & Poe, Santa Monica; Wako Works of Art, Tokyo
1997: S.L. Simpson Gallery, Toronto
1996: Friedrich Petzel Gallery, New York; neugerriemschneider, Berlin
1995: Kunstlerhaus, Stuttgart

Selected Group Exhibitions
1997: *Truce*, Site-Santa Fe, Santa Fe (curated by Francesco Bonami); 1997 Biennial Exhibition, Whitney Museum of American Art, New York (curated by L. Philips and L. Neri)
1996: *TRUE. BLISS.*, LACE, Los Angeles; *Playpen & Corpus Delirium*, Kunsthalle Zurich; *Hall of Mirrors: Art & Film since 1945*,

MOCA, Los Angeles
1995: *Interim Art*, London; Vancouver Film Festival; *La Belle et la Bête*, Musée d' Art Moderne de la Ville de Paris; *Human/Nature*, The New Museum of Contemporary Art, New York

Rut Blees Luxemburg
Born Mosel, Germany, 1967. Lives and works in London.

Selected Solo Exhibitions
1998: Kunstraum Trier
1997: Laurent Delaye Gallery, London
1995: Galerie Junge Kunst, Trier
1994: Camerawork, London

Selected Group Exhibitions
1997: *Zeitgenössische Britische Fotografie*, NGBL, Berlin; *Public Relations, New British Photography*, Stadthaus Ulm
1996: *Never Walk Alone*, Photographers' Gallery, London; *Euthanasia*, Plummet, London
1995: *Desiring Practices*, RIBA, London; *Object/Subject of Desire*, Konstfack, Stockholm; *Stream*, Plummet, London

Esko Männikkö
Born Pudasjärvi, 1959. Lives and works in Oulu, Finland.

Selected Solo Exhibitions
1997: Malmö Konsthall, Malmö; Hippolyte Photo Gallery, Helsinki; Morris Healy Gallery, New York
1996: Portikus Frankfurt; Palais des Beaux Arts, Brussels; *Mexas*, Art Pace, San Antonio
1995: *Young Artists of the Year 1995*, Tampere Art Museum, Tampere; Galerie Nordenhake, Stockholm

Selected Group Exhibitions
1997: *Truce*, Site-Santa Fe, Santa Fe (curated by Francesco Bonami); *Unknown Adventure*, Badischer Kunstverein, Karlsruhe; *Someone else with my fingerprints*, Galerie

Hauser und Wirth, Zurich
1996: *Portrett*, Museet for Samtidskunst, Oslo; *Manifesta*, Chabot Museum, Rotterdam; Sydney Biennial, Ivan Bougherty Gallery, Sydney
1995: *Art 95*, Helsinki; *Body and Soul*, Oulu; *Campo 95*, Biennale di Venezia, (curated by Francesco Bonami)

Florence Paradeis
Born Anthony, France, 1964. Lives and works in Paris.

Selected Solo Exhibitions
1997: *De Vleeshal*, Middelburg; *Institut Français*, Prague; Galerie des Archives, Paris
1996: *Mirades i Vi(ver)sions*, Fundació La Caixa, Barcelona (with Carmen Navarrete); The Showroom, London
1995: CRG Art Incorporated, New York; *Dispositif photo/vidéo*, Printemps de Cahors, Cahors, France

Selected Group Exhibitions
1997: *Vis à vi(e)s*, Galerie Art & Essai, Rennes University ; *Carte Blanche à Florence Paradeis*, Galerie des Archives, Paris: *The Great Outdoors*, Gimpel Fils, London
1996: *Campo*, Konstmuseum Malmö; *Aux limites de la Photographie*, Santiago, Chile (touring); *European Photography Award*, Bad Homburg
1995: *Images of Masculinity*, Victoria Miro, London; *Close to Life*, Third International Foto-Triennale, Esslingen; *Campo 95*, Biennale di Venezia, (curated by Francesco Bonami)

Jörg Sasse
Born Bad Salzuflen, 1962. Lives and works in Düsseldorf.

Selected Solo Exhibitions
1997: Kunsthalle Zurich; Musée

d' Art Moderne de la Ville de
Paris; Lehmann Maupin, New York
1996: Städtische Galerie Wolfsburg,
Schloss Wolfsburg; Kölnischer
Kunstverein, Cologne
1995: Galerie Wilma Tolksdorf,
Hamburg; Projekt DG Bank,
Frankfurt

Selected Group Exhibitions:
1996: *Der soziale Blick*,
Sonderausstellung Fotografie auf
der ART Frankfurt; *Fotografia
nell'arte tedesca contemporanea*,
Claudia Gian Ferrari Arte
Contemporanea, Milan and Foro
Boario, Modena
1995: Mai 36 Galerie, Zurich (with
Thomas Ruff); *Zwei und Zwanzig*,
Bonner Kunstverein, Bonn
1994: *Deutsche Kunst mit
Photographie*, Rheinisches
Landesmuseum, Bonn, Kunstverein
Wolfsburg; *De Andere, Der Andere,
L' Autre*, Werner-Mantz-Preis, Het
Nederlands Fotomuseum, Sittard,
Netherlands

Paul Seawright
Born Belfast, 1965. Lives and
works in Gwent.

Selected Solo Exhibitions
1997: Blue Sky Gallery, Portland,
Oregon; Françoise Knabe
Gallery, Frankfurt
1996: Ffotogallery, Cardiff;
Houston Fotofest
1994: Cornerhouse, Manchester

Selected Group Exhibitions
1997: Nederlands Foto Institut,
Rotterdam; *NGBK, Contemporary
British Photography*, Berlin;
IMMA/Glen Dimplex Artists Award,
Dublin
1996: *Lie of the Land*, Gallery of
Photography, Dublin (touring);
Kerlin Gallery, Dublin; *L' Imaginaire
Irlandais*, Ecole des Beaux
Arts, Paris
1995: *Ceasefire*, Wolverhampton
Museum and Art Gallery

Elisa Sighicelli
Born Turin, 1968. Lives and works
in London.

Solo Exhibitions
1996: *Arrache-coeur*, Guido Carbone
Gallery, Turin; *L' improbabile
aureola di icone metropolitane*,
Cafè Procope-Teatro Juvarra, Turin

Selected Group Exhibitions
1997: *Aperto Italia '97*, Trevi Flash
Art Museum, Trevi; *Biennale dei
Giovani Artisti dell' Europa e del
Meditterraneo*, Turin; *Proposte XII:
Ghosts of Reality*, Galleria di San
Filippo, Turin
1996: *Italians II*, Pieve di Cento,
Bologna; *Electronic-Art-Café*,
Torino-Lingotto (curated by
Achille Bonito Oliva)
1995: *Tanti auguri all' eDITOre!*,
Turin (touring exhibition for 25
years of Stampa Alternativa)

Hannah Starkey
Born Belfast, 1971. Lives and
works in London.

Solo Exhibitions
1995: Scottish Homes, Stills Gallery,
Edinburgh

Selected Group Exhibitions
1998: *Shine, Photo 98*, National
Museum of Photography, Film and
Television, Bradford
1997: *Modern Narratives*, Artsway
Ga_____ ____ ___st; *John Kobal
A_____ __al Portrait Gallery,
Lo__